ARIANA GRANDE

TWO EXTRAORDINARY PEOPLE.

CAMILA CABELLO

CONNECTED LIVES™

Ariana Grande | Camila Cabello

Ed Sheeran | Shawn Mendes

Halsey | Billie Eilish

John Legend | Michael Bublé

Kacey Musgraves | Maren Morris

Kane Brown | Sam Hunt

Kendrick Lamar | Travis Scott

Nicki Minaj | Cardi B

Photo credits: page 4: Kevin Winter / iHeartMedia via Getty Images; page 5: Ethan Miller via Getty Images; page 7: Noam Galai / Save The Children via Getty Images; page 8: Jason Merritt via Getty Images; page 9: Kevin Winter / dcp via Getty Images, Gareth Cattermole via Getty Images; page 10: Ethan Miller via Getty Images; page 11: Art Wager / E+ via Getty Images; page 12: Kevin Winter via Getty Images; page 16: Carlos Alvarez via Getty Images; page 17: Kevin Winter via Getty Images; page 18: Metro-Goldwyn-Mayer via Getty Images; page 20: Slaven Vlasic / Macy's via Getty Images; page 21: Frazer Harrison via Getty Images; page 22: Joe Corrigan via Getty Images; page 23: Kevin Winter / iHeartMedia via Getty Images; page 24: Manny Carabel via Getty Images; page 25: Gregg DeGuire via Getty Images; page 28: Kevork Djansezian via Getty Images; page 29: Mike Pont / iHeartMedia via Getty Images; page 30: Jamie McCarthy / MTV via Getty Images; page 31: Dimitrios Kambouris via Getty Images; page 32: Kevin Winter via Getty Images; page 33: Marcus Ingram via Getty Images; page 34: Chris Polk / iHeartMedia via Getty Images; page 35: Mike Coppola / iHeart via Getty Images; page 36: Frederick M. Brown via Getty Images; page 37: Tim P. Whitby / Tim P. Whitby via Getty Images; page 40: Dave Hogan / One Love Manchester via Getty Images; page 41: Nicholas Hunt / dick clark productions via Getty Images; page 44: Rich Polk / iHeartMedia via Getty Images; page 45: Christopher Polk / iHeartMedia via Getty Images; page 46: Bennett Raglin / FIJI Water via Getty Images; page 48: Rich Polk / iHeartMedia via Getty Images; page 49: Roy Rochlin / MTV via Getty Images; page 52: Kevin Winter via Getty Images; page 53: Vince Bucci / NAACP via Getty Images; page 54: Pascal Le Segretain via Getty Images; page 55: Paul Kane via Getty Images; page 56: Joe Scarnici / Qatar Airways via Getty Images; page 57: Christopher Polk / TAS via Getty Images; page 58: Dave Hogan / One Love Manchester via Getty Images; page 59: Alexander Tamargo / iHeartMedia via Getty Images; page 60: Ethan Miller / iHeartMedia via Getty Images; page 62: Christopher Polk / Coachella via Getty Images; page 63: Kevin Winter / dcp via Getty Images; page 65: Tasos Katopodis / Clear Channel via Getty Images, Theo Wargo / iHeartMedia via Getty Images; Ariana Grande head shot: Jason Merritt via Getty Images; Camila Cabello head shot: David Becker / iHeartMedia via Getty Images; background: Chris Wong / EyeEm via Getty Images

ISBN: 978-1-68021-795-7
eBook: 978-1-64598-081-0

Printed in Malaysia

24 23 22 21 20   1 2 3 4 5

TABLE OF CONTENTS

CHAPTER 1

Early Life 4

CHAPTER 2

Intro to Music 16

CHAPTER 3

Rise to Success 28

CHAPTER 4

Stardom 40

CHAPTER 5

Influences and Collaborations 52

EARLY LIFE

WHO IS ARIANA GRANDE?

Ariana Grande was born in June 1993. The singer's full name is Ariana Grande-Butera. Her family is of Italian American heritage. She is from Boca Raton, Florida. It is about an hour north of Miami. Ariana's name came from a character named Princess Oriana in *Felix the Cat: The Movie*.

WHO IS CAMILA CABELLO?

Camila Cabello is a good friend of Ariana. When she was born, her parents named her Karla Camila Cabello Estrabao. This was in March 1997. The pop star is of Cuban and Mexican heritage. Her birthplace is Cojímar, Cuba. As a child, she spent time in both Havana and Mexico City. When the future star was six, she moved to Florida. Her family still lives in Miami.

THE GRANDE FAMILY

Before she was born, Ariana's parents lived in New York City. Edward Butera is her father. He is a graphic designer from New Jersey. Ariana's mother is Joan Grande. Joan is CEO of a communication and alarm system company. She is from Brooklyn. When Ariana was young, the couple divorced. This has made the star feel torn between her parents. "Even years later, I'm still in the middle," she told *Billboard*.

New York City, New York

Camila with her mother

THE ESTRABAO FAMILY

Camila's father, Alejandro, is from Mexico. Sinuhe, her mother, is Cuban. When Camila was six, her mother said they were going to Disney World. Instead, the two emigrated from Mexico. They spent a day in a holding center in Texas. Then, after a 36-hour bus ride, they arrived in Miami. A friend took them in. After more than a year, Alejandro came to Florida. Camila became a U.S. citizen in 2008.

Frankie Grande

AN ENTERTAINING BROTHER

Ariana grew up with an older half-brother. Frankie was the first performer in the family. His musical theater career took him to Broadway in 2007. In 2014, he was a contestant on the reality TV show *Big Brother*. He has worked as both a performer and a producer. As a child, Ariana enjoyed watching him. Now the two support each other's careers.

SINGING SISTERS

Camila grew up with a sibling too. Her younger sister is Sofia Cabello. Sofia was born in 2007. Like Camila, she enjoys singing. Fans often see the two talk on social media. The sisters sing together, and Camila posts Sofia's pictures. They sometimes perform covers of *High School Musical* songs. On TikTok, Sofia often lip-syncs to Camila's songs.

A WEIRD LITTLE GIRL

Ariana told *Billboard* she was "a very weird little girl."
She had her own interests. For example, she liked to
wear skeleton face paint even when it wasn't Halloween.
For one birthday, the singer had a *Jaws*-themed party.
Her friends were scared of the decorations, she said.

Miami, Florida

LEARNING ENGLISH

When Camila arrived in Miami, she felt different too. She spoke no English at all. Cartoons helped her learn. "I never thought about it when I was little, but there is something shocking about moving to a new country and not speaking the language," she said to the *Guardian*. On her first day of school, the six-year-old was asked if she spoke English. Her answer was yes. The truth was, Spanish was her only language.

THE ACTING BUG

Ariana began singing and acting at an early age. It was a family activity. Joan, Frankie, and Ariana were all part of local productions of *Annie* and *The Wizard of Oz*. In both plays, Ariana played the lead. Her mother told the *South Florida Sun-Sentinel*, "It was the most rewarding time I've spent with her."

When it came to acting, Ariana was a perfectionist. She was a hard worker too. "I just wanted to do every single show," she told *Billboard*.

VERY SHY

"I had a drama-free upbringing," Camila told *People*. "But it was at times a little boring." Her extreme shyness may have played a part in that. Pushing herself was hard. She lacked self-confidence. Unlike Ariana, she never put herself out there. The singer says shyness made her miss out on experiences. Over the years, she has worked to realize her inner strength.

LEARNING LANGUAGE THROUGH MEDIA

Camila learned some of her English through television. Many people learn foreign languages through television and movies. Subtitles and repetitive storylines can help. Music is also a great tool to learn a new language. Non-native speakers tend to have clearer accents when they sing in foreign languages. This is partly because singing is slower than talking, so accents can be heard better. Singing new words makes them easier to remember, according to research.

BEST FRIENDS

Ariana still has a group of close friends from growing up. One is Alexa Luria. The two often interact on social media. They have traveled together. Ariana even got an "A" tattoo in Alexa's honor. The singer was extremely close to her mother growing up too. "She's the most . . . independent woman you'll ever meet—not the cookies-in-the-oven type," the star said to *Complex*.

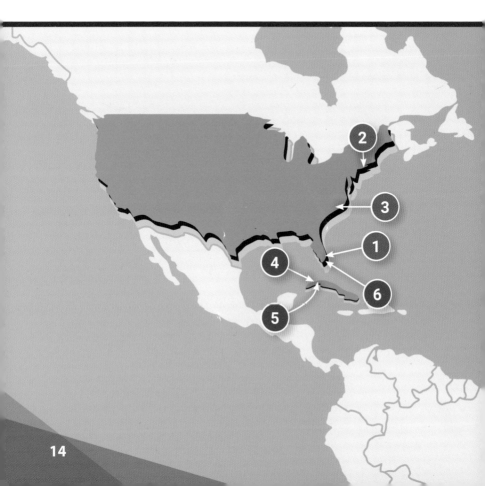

A BOOKWORM

As a child, Camila was a bookworm. She read all the time. The singer also described her younger self as having a big imagination. At school Camila "was kind of invisible," she told *People*. Then acting and singing entered her life. An eighth-grade theater teacher offered encouragement. After Camila was famous, the two got back in touch.

ARIANA GRANDE

1. **Boca Raton, Florida:** This is where Ariana was born.
2. **New York City, New York:** Her first professional role was on Broadway in 2008.
3. **Silver Spring, Maryland:** In 2013, this was the first stop on Ariana's first tour.

CAMILA CABELLO

4. **Havana, Cuba:** Camila was born in the Cuban capital.
5. **Cojímar, Cuba:** This is where she spent her early childhood.
6. **Miami, Florida:** When she was six, Camila moved here with her mother.

CHAPTER 2

INTRO TO MUSIC

GLORIA ESTEFAN

Ariana always knew she wanted to sing. Famous Cuban American singer Gloria Estefan was an early inspiration. When Ariana was eight, she was singing karaoke on a cruise ship. Estefan was in the audience. Afterward, the star encouraged her, Ariana said on *Alan Carr: Chatty Man*. "I just want to let you know that you are so talented and do not ever give up," Ariana remembers Estefan saying.

Gloria Estefan

SPANISH MUSIC AND GUITAR

Camila has stated her love for Gloria Estefan too. She grew up listening to Latin American music. One of her favorite singers was Cuban megastar Celia Cruz. Another was Mexican singer Alejandro Fernández. In seventh grade, the future star began to play guitar. "Initially, I taught myself," she explained to *Marie Claire*. "The first song I ever learned to play was 'Stuck in the Moment,' by Justin Bieber." Her father also plays guitar and has a strong voice.

Alejandro Fernández

AN EARLY SINGER

The first song Ariana remembers singing is "Somewhere Over the Rainbow." Her favorite movie was *The Wizard of Oz*. The father of her theater friend Misha was a record producer. "[Ariana] could sing like Mariah Carey even back then," he told the *Palm Beach Post*. When she was eight, Ariana first appeared on television. She sang the national anthem at a Florida Panthers hockey game.

The Wizard of Oz

A SHY SINGER

Camila was not ready for the spotlight as early as Ariana. At Camila's fourth-grade choir audition, she was anxious. The singer forgot the words and didn't make the cut. Despite her talent, Camila rarely sang in front of people. "She was so shy, so shy," her mother told the *New York Times*. "We didn't even think music was a possibility for her." Camila wouldn't even sing in front of her family.

SOUTH FLORIDA MUSICIANS

Many famous musicians are from the busy Miami area. Jason Derulo was born in Miami in 1989. He went to a performing arts high school there. Several famous Miamians even have Cuban heritage, just like Camila. Pitbull was born in Miami. His family is Cuban American. Gloria Estefan immigrated from Cuba when she was young. This world-famous pop star graduated from University of Miami. Yet another Cuban American singer born in Miami is Camila's Fifth Harmony bandmate, Lauren Jauregui.

SONGWRITING

Ariana learned how to read music while playing the French horn. She could also play a bit of piano. At a young age, she started writing songs on GarageBand. This is a computer program for making music. In an interview with music website Neon Limelight, she talked about her early songs. "The first song I ever wrote was really silly, and I still actually have it on my computer," Ariana said. "It was about rain. Like, just about rain. No deeper meaning . . . just rain."

Fifth Harmony

THE X FACTOR

Camila slowly started to reveal her singing talent. She
posted a few YouTube videos. Her face was always
hidden while she sang, though. In 2012, Camila finally
decided to commit to her passion. For her birthday,
she asked her mom to drive her 15 hours away. It was
to audition for *The X Factor* in North Carolina. At first,
producers made her an alternate. This meant she could
only sing for the judges if there was time. "I ended up
auditioning because they saw how badly I wanted it and
how persistent I was—it's a Cuban thing," she said on
Lena Dunham's podcast. Aretha Franklin's "Respect"
was her audition song. When it was over, she knew that
music was her future.

The cast of *13*

FROM MIDDLE SCHOOL TO BROADWAY

When Ariana was 15 years old, she made it to Broadway. It was 2008. She had landed the role of Charlotte in the musical *13*. The role won her a National Youth Theatre Award. To go from school to a full-time job was a major change. "That was a really crazy transition to make because it was so much hard work," she told Neon Limelight.

FIFTH HARMONY

Like Ariana, Camila found success at the age of 15 too. First she faced a minor setback, though. After getting on *The X Factor*, she was cut early on. It was during the show's "boot camp." But judge Simon Cowell saw something in her. Camila was "super talented, ambitious, [and] very passionate," he told *Variety*. Cowell and the other judges formed a girl band called Fifth Harmony. The band included Camila and four other contestants. They competed on the show, finishing third. Soon after, Fifth Harmony signed a joint record deal. It was with Simon Cowell's label Syco Records and Epic Records.

Fifth Harmony

NICKELODEON

After her Broadway work, Ariana was cast on a Nickelodeon show. She played Cat Valentine in *VICTORiOUS*. It ran from 2010 until early 2013. The show was set at a performing arts high school. Singing was part of Ariana's role. Cat Valentine became a popular character. After the show ended, there was a spin-off called *Sam & Cat*. This was also a spin-off of *iCarly*. Ariana starred on the show until it ended in 2014.

VICTORIOUS

Ariana was part of the beloved but short-lived Nickelodeon show *VICTORiOUS*. This wacky comedy was set in a performing arts high school in Hollywood. The future star played Cat, a sensitive and scatterbrained character. She was best friends with the main character, Tori Vega. Victoria Justice played Tori. Ariana is still friends with many of the cast members. A few of them even performed in her "Thank U, Next" video.

Victoria Justice

THE X FACTOR

This show started in the United Kingdom. It was created by Simon Cowell of *American Idol* fame. The title refers to the unknown "something" that makes someone a star. Unlike *American Idol*, this show relies on coaching and mentoring. In that way, it is similar to *The Voice*. The world-famous boy band One Direction was formed on the show. They placed third during their season, just like Fifth Harmony.

Simon Cowell

DROPPING OUT OF SCHOOL

Camila had been taught to take risks. "The way my mom raised me, it has always been: Don't settle. Jump and hope you grow wings on the way down," she told *Billboard*. Soon after *The X Factor*, Camila took another big jump. During the 2012–2013 school year, the singer left school. She followed her show-business dreams with Fifth Harmony. After homeschooling for the rest of high school, she earned her diploma.

BRANCHING OUT

In 2011, Ariana took a risk too. People already knew her from *VICTORiOUS*. Still, she wanted to do more with music than a *VICTORiOUS* soundtrack. Acting was fun, "but music has always been first and foremost with me," she told *Rolling Stone*. Ariana had opened a YouTube account in 2007. Now she began uploading many songs. The risk was a success. Her covers of Rihanna, Mariah Carey, and others got over 10 million views. That was before she was even offered a record deal.

MORE FIFTH HARMONY

At first, Camila loved being in Fifth Harmony. "I was so excited that it wasn't over because I wanted to just keep going on that journey. . . . I was like a kid in a candy store," Camila told Lena Dunham in her podcast. However, she soon started feeling frustrated. There was not enough freedom. She did not want to keep singing songs someone else wrote.

PARALLEL LIVES

Born in Florida

Spoke English as her first language

Loved performing from a young age

Born in the 1990s

Sings in soprano voice

Has a sibling who is also into music
and performing

Lived in South Florida

Born in Cuba

Spoke Spanish as her first language

Was shy as a child

CHAPTER 3

RISE TO SUCCESS

SIGNING A CONTRACT

In August 2011, Ariana signed a contract with Republic Records. That December, she put out her first single. It was a peppy song called "Put Your Hearts Up." In 2013, she released *Yours Truly*. She was only 20. The album debuted at number one on the Billboard 200. "The Way" was a top-ten single. Critics thought Ariana's voice was very strong. "I didn't realize how much more enjoyable it is to sing words that you've written," Ariana told Neon Limelight.

FIFTH HARMONY'S HUGE SUCCESS

Ariana's record contract put her in the spotlight. Upon joining Fifth Harmony, the same happened to Camila. She became very busy. An EP called *Better Together* came out in 2013. It landed at number six on the Billboard 200. Soon after, Fifth Harmony toured with Demi Lovato. They also had their own tour. The group even got to perform twice at the White House. By December 2016, their songs had been streamed 1.6 billion times in the U.S.

NO PROBLEM

On April 27, 2014, Ariana released the song "Problem."
It had a guest verse from rapper Iggy Azalea. The single
was a smash hit. In only 37 minutes, it reached the top
of the iTunes chart. This broke a record held by Taylor
Swift. "Problem" was one of the best-selling singles ever.
Ariana won her first MTV Video Music Award (VMA) for
the song.

DISTINGUISHING HERSELF

Fifth Harmony's album *Reflection* came out in 2015. Their debut was a hit, just as Ariana's had been. In 2016, they put out another hit. This was 7/27. They became the most successful girl group since Destiny's Child. Up to 2016, the group sold more than 7 million digital songs. Camila was the fan favorite for her voice and look. She also sang the most of all the members.

SECOND ALBUM

In 2014, Ariana released her second studio album. *My Everything* was its title. Her hit song "Problem" was on the track list. "Bang Bang" was too. This was a song with Jessie J and Nicki Minaj. It was Ariana's third-straight top-five hit that year. Her risks were paying off. "Everything that I was terrified to try and was absolutely positive I would hate, I tried," the singer told *Billboard*. For example, hit songwriter Max Martin suggested she sing a little ahead of the beat on "Break Free." She loved the result.

Nicki Minaj

Machine Gun Kelly

BRANCHING OUT

Camila was the first Fifth Harmony member to release music under her own name. Like Ariana, the ambitious singer wanted to find her own voice. She attended writing sessions with famous producers like Diplo and Benny Blanco. In 2015, "I Know What You Did Last Summer" was released. This song features Shawn Mendes. Machine Gun Kelly rapped on "Bad Things." The duet was a huge hit in 2016. It was nominated for a Billboard Music Award and won a Radio Disney Music Award.

FIRST TOUR

Ariana started her first arena tour in 2015. The Honeymoon Tour was for *My Everything*. It was an elaborate show. There were many costume changes. Stars like Childish Gambino and Nicki Minaj appeared on video screens. "I want to make sure that my fans have the best night of their lives," Ariana said in a video that opened the show.

NOT IN HARMONY

Camila asked to help write lyrics for Fifth Harmony songs. The group refused. They wouldn't allow her to work on a solo album either. "I was just curious and I wanted to learn and I saw all these people around me making music, writing songs and being so free," she told the *New York Times*. "I just wanted to do that and it did not work."

JUST GETTING STARTED

In 2016, Ariana's third album came out. "Dangerous Woman" was the lead single. It was also the name of the album. The single broke an important record. Ariana was the first artist to have her first three lead singles start in the Billboard Hot 100's top ten. On the album, Ariana sang about finding herself. *Dangerous Woman* was hugely successful. She felt she could do even better. "I feel like I'm still just getting started—a lot of people forget I'm only three years in," she said to *Billboard*.

SOLO ACTS WHO STARTED IN GROUPS

Many megastars got their start as part of a singing group. Michael Jackson was part of his family's band, the Jackson Five. Justin Timberlake was in boy band NSYNC. Beyoncé was part of the successful girl group Destiny's Child. They learned the business and gained recognition through these experiences.

Justin Timberlake

LEAVING FIFTH HARMONY

Fifth Harmony put out a statement on December 18, 2016. They said Camila was leaving the group. Another statement said she did not attend group meetings. Camila was surprised. She said they released the statement without her knowing. "If anyone wants to explore their individuality, it's not right for people to tell you no," Camila told the *New York Times*. Still, the singer and her manager admit that the band helped her grow. Her solo career was about to take off.

FAMILY SUPPORT

Ariana's rise to success was fast. She credits her family, especially her mother, for helping her stay focused and happy. "It hasn't gone to my head or anything, but my mom has made me feel important since I was just a bumblebee in *Billy Goats Gruff* in my school production," the singer told Neon Limelight. Her mother always supported her. There was no pressure to be a star, though.

HARD WORK AND LOVE

Camila's family was also important to her success. They taught her to work hard. In Cuba, her mother was an architect. In Miami, she stocked shoes at Marshalls. Alejandro washed cars. The family kept working. Eventually, they started their own construction company. "If we had food to eat, a roof over our heads and I was going to school, that was enough," Camila told *Teen Vogue*. She still lives in Miami. The singer's mother often goes to her concerts.

CAREER MILESTONES

1993
Ariana is born.

1997
Camila is born.

2003
Camila and her mother immigrate to the United States.

2010
Ariana is cast as Cat Valentine on the Nickelodeon show *VICTORiOUS*.

2012
Fifth Harmony is formed.

2016
Dangerous Woman is released.

2017
A bombing occurs at Ariana's Manchester concert on May 22. She delays the rest of her tour.

2017
"Crying in the Club" is released. It's Camila's first solo single.

2018
Sweetener comes out. NPR includes the album on its "Best Albums of 2018" list. In November, Ariana releases "Thank U, Next." The single stays at number one for seven weeks.

2018
Camila, her first solo album, comes out.

CHAPTER 4

STARDOM

MANCHESTER

On May 22, 2017, Ariana had a show in Manchester. A bomber killed 22 people at the concert. It was the worst terrorist attack in England since 2005. Ariana was seriously affected by the attack. She has said she suffers from post-traumatic stress disorder (PTSD). In a letter to her fans, she wrote, "Music . . . is comfort. . . . It is happiness. It is the last thing that would ever harm someone. . . . When something so opposite and so poisonous takes place . . . it is shocking and heartbreaking in a way that seems impossible to fully recover from."

FINDING HERSELF

Camila's first solo single came out in May 2017. "Crying in the Club" did not do well. Instead of leading her first album, it was cut. "That song . . . doesn't feel or sound like Camila," her manager told the *New York Times*. "We were most successful when Camila trusted in her own instincts." Producer Frank Dukes had worked with Drake and Lorde. He encouraged Camila. Soon, she discovered her style. It is influenced by the Latin music she loves.

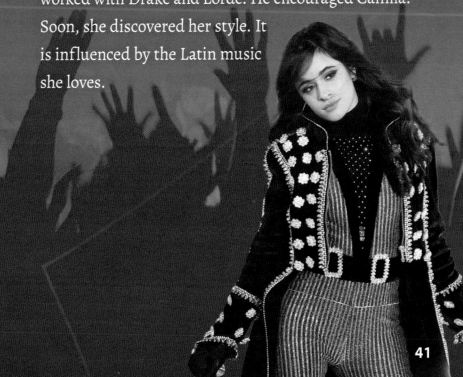

PTSD AND OCD

After the Manchester bombing, Ariana developed PTSD. On Instagram, she posted a brain scan that she said showed changes in her brain. Camila has obsessive-compulsive disorder (OCD). "If I get really stressed thinking about something, I'll start to have the same thought over and over again, and . . . I feel like something bad is about to happen if I don't keep thinking about it," she told *Cosmopolitan UK*.

ONE LOVE

Two weeks after the bombing, Ariana organized the One Love Manchester Benefit Concert. It raised money for the We Love Manchester Emergency Fund. The concert included Justin Bieber, Miley Cyrus, Coldplay, and Katy Perry. Camila sent a video message in support of her friend. Ariana sang "Somewhere Over the Rainbow" at the show. She donated proceeds from the recording to the emergency fund. The singer raised $13 million for victims and their families.

"HAVANA"

Frank Dukes inspired Camila's first hit single. She and the producer were hanging out, eating sushi. He played her a piece of music he wrote. Its salsa style reminded Camila of Havana. The singer wrote the chorus right away. "Havana" features the rapper Young Thug. It topped the Billboard Pop Songs radio airplay chart for seven weeks. In 2018, the song held Spotify's record for most-streamed song by a female artist. *Pitchfork* called "Havana" part of Camila's "superstar origin story." The star was born.

BIGGEST BENEFIT CONCERTS

The first large benefit concert was thrown by Beatles member George Harrison and Ravi Shankar in 1971. It was for refugees from East Pakistan. Some other famous benefit concerts include Live Aid in 1985 and the Freddie Mercury Tribute Concert for AIDS Awareness in 1992. America: A Tribute to Heroes in 2001 and Live Earth in 2007 raised many millions of dollars and important awareness for their causes.

SWEETENER

Ariana's star continued to rise in 2018. Her fourth album, *Sweetener*, was released in August. Lead single "No Tears Left to Cry" was a top-ten hit. A new single, "Thank U, Next," was released soon after the album. This surprise single was another record-breaking hit. It broke Spotify's record for single-day streams twice. The song was Ariana's first number-one single on the Hot 100. Critics praised "Thank U, Next" for its positive message.

CAMILA

The success of "Havana" changed Camila's direction.
"There were songs that five months ago were my favorite
songs, and then two weeks after [we] scrapped it from the
album," Camila told *Rolling Stone*. Originally, the album
was called *The Hurting. The Healing. The Loving.* Then the
title was changed to *Camila*. She wrote or cowrote every
song. Released in January 2018, *Camila* was as successful
as Ariana's albums. It topped the charts. The singer was
the youngest to do this with a debut since Shawn Mendes
in 2015.

THANK U, NEXT

On November 30, 2018, the video for "Thank U, Next" came out. It referenced *Legally Blonde, Bring It On, 13 Going on 30*, and *Mean Girls*. Actors from the original films were in it. The video had over 55 million views in 24 hours. This broke a YouTube record. In February 2019, the album *Thank U, Next* was released. This was just months after *Sweetener* came out. Ariana's fourth number-one album had the biggest week of streaming ever for a pop album. She released five albums in six years. Each one went platinum.

BECOMING ESTABLISHED

The year 2018 was a big year for Camila too. In April, the Never Be the Same Tour began. It was her first as a solo artist. That year also marked her solo arrival on award show stages. At the 2018 Grammys, she spoke out onstage about immigration. The singer took home two VMAs in August 2018. At the show, she met up with Ariana, who won an award too. Later that year, Camila was nominated for her first two Grammys. They were Best Pop Solo Performance and Best Pop Vocal Album.

TOUR BUSES

Touring is where musicians make most of their money. Many perform more than a hundred times per year. Traveling by tour bus is more convenient than flying. Most have a living room, kitchen, and sleeping area. The bus usually expands when it's parked, sliding out to become wider. John Legend's bus has a gourmet kitchen. Mariah Carey's has a marble staircase leading to a second story. Ariana calls her touring crew a "really beautiful family."

ONE, TWO, AND THREE

The single "7 Rings" entered the charts at number one in February 2019. It was just three weeks after "Thank U, Next" left the spot. Ariana soon reached a new level of superstardom. She was the first artist since the Beatles to have songs in the top three spots on the Hot 100 at the same time. "Thank U, Next," "Break Up with Your Girlfriend, I'm Bored," and "7 Rings" were all on the chart together. Her star power was felt on social media too. As of September 2019, she was the most-followed woman on Instagram. Overall, the singer was the second-most-followed person.

CONTINUED SUCCESS

Camila won two VMAs in 2019. She also performed at the awards show with Shawn Mendes. Their performance made headlines. It was the first time the pair had performed "Señorita" live together. The singer branched out into acting too. In April 2019, it was announced that Camila would star as Cinderella in an upcoming movie. "It's honestly a dream for me. And also a little bit terrifying," she told *Variety*. The star is taking acting classes for the role. In September 2019, Camila announced a second full-length album, *Romance*.

Shawn Mendes

GIVING BACK

Ariana gives back to causes she believes in. As a girl, she and her mother formed a theater group called Kids Who Care. The group sang at charity events. Later, the singer donated her money from concerts. One was for victims of violence at the 2017 white nationalist rally in Charlottesville, Virginia. Another was for Planned Parenthood. Both Camila and Ariana are vegans. They also care about the environment. The stars each used their social media platforms to spread awareness of the 2019 Amazon rain forest fires.

TOP BILLBOARD HOT 100 SINGLES

● ARIANA GRANDE

#2	Problem featuring Iggy Azalea	6/2014
#3	Bang Bang featuring Nicki Minaj, Jessie J	10/2014
#1	Thank U, Next	11/2018
#1	7 Rings	2/2019
#2	Break Up with Your Girlfriend, I'm Bored	2/2019

DOING HER PART

In 2016, Camila worked with Save the Children. She designed a "Love Only" T-shirt. Her important social media messages end with those words. The T-shirt was sold to raise money for girls' education and health care. Another group she has worked with is the Children's Health Fund. It provides health care to poor families. In 2017, the singer and Lin-Manuel Miranda released "Almost Like Praying." The song raised funds for the victims of Hurricane Maria in Puerto Rico.

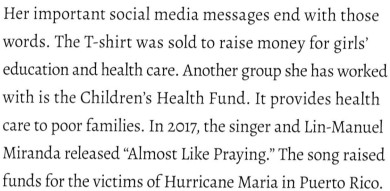

CAMILA CABELLO

#20	I Know What You Did Last Summer featuring Shawn Mendes	1/2016
#4	Bad Things featuring Machine Gun Kelly	2/2017
#1	Havana featuring Young Thug	1/2018
#6	Never Be the Same	5/2018
#1	Señorita featuring Shawn Mendes	8/2019

CHAPTER 5

INFLUENCES AND COLLABORATIONS

WOMEN'S VOICES

Ariana has always loved female singers with strong voices. She told *Billboard* she is Imogen Heap's "number-one fan. . . . I just can't get enough of her." India Arie, Judy Garland, and Brandy were other childhood favorites. When she was 14, Ariana wanted to make a soul album like India Arie. Whitney Houston "inspired me to start singing as a little girl," she told *Billboard*.

Brandy

LATIN MUSICIANS

Camila was mostly influenced by Latin music as a child. Like Ariana, she loves many female musicians. "Women are powerful and music as a form of expression allows you to take ownership of that. . . . Imagine Beyoncé commanding a massive stage—I don't think anything can rival that in terms of an expression of women's empowerment," Camila told *Hello!* magazine. She went on to say that any woman in her life can inspire her, from a fan to her little sister.

Beyoncé

MARIAH CAREY AND MADONNA

Songwriter Savan Kotecha has worked with Ariana on many songs. "What makes an Ariana song an Ariana song is that it's a song no one else can sing," he said to *Billboard*. She is known for her incredible technique. People often compare her to other singers with huge range and control. The most common are Mariah Carey and Whitney Houston.

Ariana told Neon Limelight, "As far as vocal influences go, Whitney and Mariah pretty much cover it." Madonna is also a hero. "She is strength, she is freedom, she is wisdom beyond anybody's comprehension," Ariana told *Billboard*.

Madonna

Ed Sheeran

A RANGE OF INFLUENCES

Camila admires many different singers. Some are Michael Jackson, Bruno Mars, and Rihanna. Others are reggaeton stars like Calle 13 and J Balvin. Reggaeton is a mix of hip-hop and Caribbean music. One of Camila's biggest idols is singer-songwriter Ed Sheeran. The star said she cried when she met him. "He's incredible at putting love, emotion, and feeling into words," she said to radio station Capital FM. Literature also inspires the singer. For example, she loves Rupi Kaur's poetry book *Milk and Honey*. Gabriel García Márquez's novel *Love in the Time of Cholera* is another favorite.

DESTINY'S CHILD

Like Camila, Ariana deeply admires Beyoncé. She began listening to the megastar when she sang with Destiny's Child. "That's where I discovered my range. I grew up listening to Destiny's Child. I would try so hard to mimic all Beyoncé's little runs and ad-lib things. They are so precise. It's like math," she said to *V* magazine.

MARIAH CAREY

Singer Mariah Carey has been famous since the 1990s, when her first album topped the charts. She was named the Best-Selling Female Artist of the Millennium at the World Music Awards in 2000. Carey has released 15 albums and won five Grammys. The singer is one of the creators of modern R&B. Her voice is distinctive, and she has an incredible five-octave range. Many trills and runs are featured in her songs.

Mariah Carey

Charli XCX

Taylor Swift

TAYLOR SWIFT

Camila said that she had a poster of Taylor Swift in her childhood bedroom. Now the two are friends. She has even opened for Swift on tour. "I love her. We just talk about boys," Camila explained to *Cosmopolitan UK*. "She loves love, and we love talking about it. It's fun to just vent and talk and dream."

Victoria Monét

VICTORIA MONÉT

Ariana often works with songwriter Victoria Monét. They met while Ariana was on Nickelodeon. The star has said Monét is her best friend. Monét cowrote the hit songs "Thank U, Next" and "7 Rings." She was even in both videos. Kendrick Lamar and Janelle Monáe have released songs written by Monét. A solo musician herself, Monét has opened for Ariana. She also opened for Fifth Harmony when Camila was in the group.

SHAWN MENDES

Camila has long-running musical partners too. One is Shawn Mendes. The two cowrote and performed the song "Señorita." It was released in June 2019. "Señorita" was a huge global hit. The song broke Spotify's record as the biggest single-day debut of a male/female duet ever. "It would take a big force to stop her from taking over the world," Mendes said to *Billboard*.

Shawn Mendes

Childish Gambino

FEATURED GUESTS

Ariana often has featured guests on her albums. "Break Your Heart Right Back" features Childish Gambino. This is one of Ariana's favorite songs from *My Everything*. "Best Mistake" with Big Sean is also from that album. It helped the singer break yet another record. The song made her the first female artist to have three top-six songs on the Billboard Digital Songs Chart at the same time.

MANY COLLABORATORS

Pitbull and J Balvin joined Camila for "Hey Ma." This was for the *Fate of the Furious* soundtrack. The song has a Spanish and an English version. It got a Latin Grammy nomination. Camila worked with Charli XCX and Quavo on "OMG." Ed Sheeran cowrote "The Boy." They recorded a version together, but it was not released. This song was discarded from her planned first album, *Camila*. The singer has also been featured on "Sangria Wine" by Pharrell Williams.

WHISTLE REGISTER

Camila and Ariana are both sopranos. That means their voices are high. Ariana also has the whistle register. This is an extremely high mode of the human voice. It's even higher than the falsetto register. Few people have it, as it is created by a different part of the vocal cords than normal singing. Mariah Carey and Christina Aguilera are other stars who can use the whistle register.

CAMRIANA

Camila and Ariana have been close friends since 2013.
Their fans call them "Camriana." They met at MTV's
Artist to Watch concert in 2013. Both Camila and Ariana
are featured on Cashmere Cat's album 9. Ariana has
said she loves singing with Camila. In 2018, the pair
posted a YouTube video of themselves singing in a car.
On Twitter, the friends are often seen joking with and
sending support to each other.

SUPPORTIVE FRIENDS

Ariana has wished Camila success. "When my first songs came out, she FaceTimed me and was like 'Congratulations, I'm so proud of you,'" Camila said on *This Morning*. It's a mutual feeling. In 2017, Camila went to a Dangerous Woman show in California. The singers choose support over competition.

SHARED COLLABORATIONS

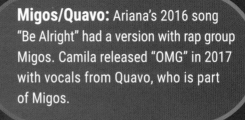

Cashmere Cat: Ariana has been on two of his songs, "Adore" in 2015 and "Quit" in 2017. Camila was on "Love Incredible" in 2017. It was her first single after Fifth Harmony.

Migos/Quavo: Ariana's 2016 song "Be Alright" had a version with rap group Migos. Camila released "OMG" in 2017 with vocals from Quavo, who is part of Migos.

Young Thug: Ariana worked with the rapper on a Calvin Harris song, "Heatstroke." Camila's "Havana" has a guest spot with rapper Young Thug.

Troye Sivan: Ariana was featured on his song "Dance to This." Camila is friends with the singer Troye Sivan.

CONNECTED LIVES

Camila and Ariana are sure to continue helping each other and other female musicians too. Sisterhood in the music industry is important to them. It makes a difficult job more about collaboration than competition. This is happening in many industries as women decide to stand up for each other.

TAKE A LOOK INSIDE

ED SHEERAN

TWO EXTRAORDINARY PEOPLE.

SHAWN MENDES

CHAPTER 1

EARLY LIFE

WHO IS ED SHEERAN?

Ed Sheeran is an English singer-songwriter. He performs with an acoustic guitar and no band. The singer was born in February 1991. Ed grew up in Framlingham, Suffolk. This is a small town in eastern England. Fewer than 4,000 people live there.

WHO IS SHAWN MENDES?

Shawn Mendes is a Canadian singer. Like Ed Sheeran, he writes his own songs. The singer was born in Toronto, Ontario, in August 1998. His parents raised him in Pickering, a suburb of Toronto. He told *Rolling Stone* that it is "the most comforting place in the world." Even after becoming a star, Shawn lived at home.

4

5

FULLY COMMITTED

Ed soon knew he only wanted to make music. Between 2007 and 2016, the singer says he never took a day off. He wrote music or performed every day. His parents helped him make professional albums and merchandise. They also took him to local gigs. "As a teenager my first dream was to make enough money from music to pay the rent and sell 100 CDs," he told GQ UK.

GOOFING AROUND

While Ed had ambitions, Shawn's music life was mostly for fun at first. In early 2013, Shawn joined the now-defunct social media site Vine. This site allowed users to upload six-second videos. These short clips played on a loop. Shawn's first videos on the platform were the kind of videos many teens post. A shot of his face in a dark room was his first Vine. "My #firstpost on Vine," the caption read.

PARALLEL LIVES

Bullied in school
Has an older brother
Family was musical
From England

Born in the 1990s
Middle-class upbringing
Sibling is also into music and performing
Got started by singing at school
Plays guitar

Played sports
School was pretty easy for him
Has a younger sister
From Canada

GIVING BACK

Ed says all he wants is enough money to be comfortable. In 2014, he donated many of his clothes to thrift stores. Much of his money goes to children's hospitals. Family and friends also receive generous gifts. The star raises money playing shows and recording music. Ed was part of Band Aid 30 in 2014. It raised money for the Ebola crisis in western Africa.

A FORCE FOR GOOD

Shawn helps people too. One way is through social media. He raised funds for the Red Cross after the 2017 Mexico City earthquake. Together with his label, the singer donated $100,000 to the cause. Through a campaign with DoSomething.org, Shawn aimed to raise kids' self-esteem. In 2015, he sold exclusive items to raise money to build a new school in Ghana. His #BuildASchoolWithShawn campaign reached its goal in only a week.

EQUIVALENT ALBUM SALES
(AS OF LATE 2018)

Fans buy physical copies and digital copies of an album. They also stream the album and its songs. Digital purchases are another way fans can listen to albums. Equivalent Album Sales add up all of these ways of accessing music.

+ *(Plus)* 2,590,526
× *(Multiply)* 7,244,624
÷ *(Divide)* 9,631,543

Handwritten 3,000,460
Illuminate 3,663,560
Shawn Mendes 1,028,554

FOR MORE TITLES AND INFORMATION ⟶

CONNECTED LIVES™